BEVERLEY MINSTER

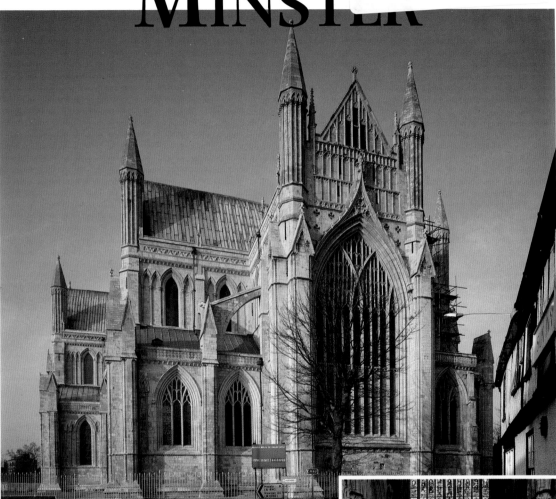

Contents

Above:
The Early English east end of the Minster with 15th-century Perpendicular alterations including the Great East Window and gable.

Right:
The sanctuary and Great East Window.

Introduction

Beverley Minster is built on the scale of a cathedral, and it is in the view of many architectural writers finer than some churches which are cathedrals: for instance, it has been judged by Alec Clifton-Taylor 'the finest non-cathedral church in the kingdom' after Westminster Abbey. Many visitors are surprised to find such a magnificent building in a small town like Beverley, especially as the town also includes the imposing church of St Mary. The reasons are simple: Beverley was not a small town by medieval standards, and the Minster was not a mere parish church but a wealthy collegiate church and a centre for pilgrims. Most of the building we see today was built between 1220 and 1400, and it was during that period (in 1377) that Beverley was taxed as the eleventh largest town in England.

The word 'Minster' is a source of much confusion. It is a translation of the Latin word *monasterium*, 'monastery', but in Anglo-Saxon times it was also used to mean any large church served by a body of priests; the term is still popularly used for other great churches in the region which had cathedral or college status, such as York, Lincoln, Howden, Ripon and Southwell. Beverley was founded for monks, but from the 10th to the 16th centuries it was staffed by a regulated group of priests who served the town and the surrounding area. In 1548 the Crown seized most of the Minster's revenues, in a suppression of colleges comparable to the dissolution of the monasteries, and reduced it to the status of a parish church. Neglect of the fabric through lack of funds nearly caused disaster, but fortunately major restorations since the 18th century have saved it, and it still stands today, combining its parochial functions with being effectively, as it was intended, a sub-cathedral in the large diocese of York.

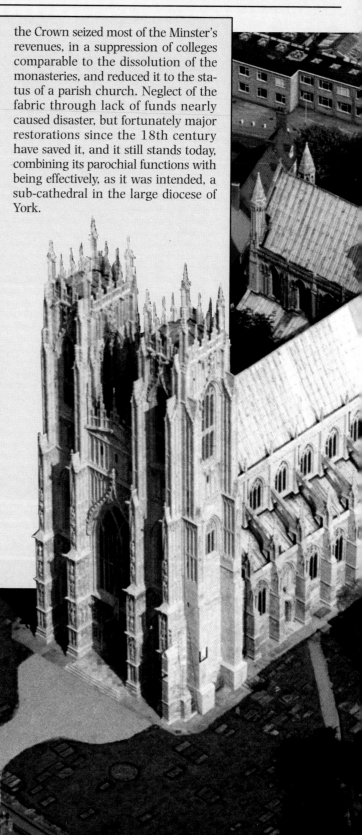

Foreword from the Vicar and Churchwardens

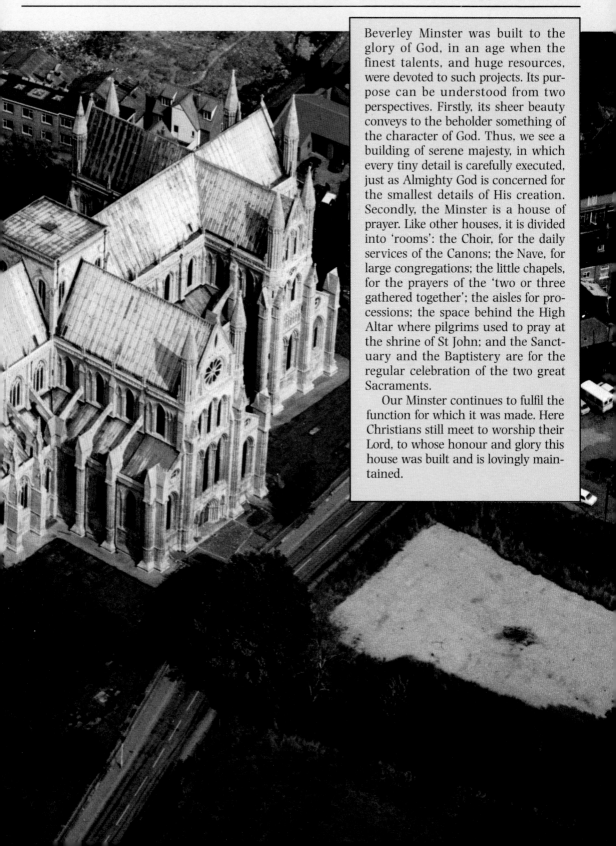

Beverley Minster was built to the glory of God, in an age when the finest talents, and huge resources, were devoted to such projects. Its purpose can be understood from two perspectives. Firstly, its sheer beauty conveys to the beholder something of the character of God. Thus, we see a building of serene majesty, in which every tiny detail is carefully executed, just as Almighty God is concerned for the smallest details of His creation. Secondly, the Minster is a house of prayer. Like other houses, it is divided into 'rooms': the Choir, for the daily services of the Canons; the Nave, for large congregations; the little chapels, for the prayers of the 'two or three gathered together'; the aisles for processions; the space behind the High Altar where pilgrims used to pray at the shrine of St John; and the Sanctuary and the Baptistery are for the regular celebration of the two great Sacraments.

Our Minster continues to fulfil the function for which it was made. Here Christians still meet to worship their Lord, to whose honour and glory this house was built and is lovingly maintained.

We know very little about the origins of Beverley and its Minster except for what St Bede tells us in his *Ecclesiastical History of the English People*, completed in 731. There is evidence for Roman and prehistoric settlement in the area, but Bede implies that the district was uninhabited when Bishop John of York (706–c.714) founded a monastery called Inderawuda. The name means 'in the wood of Deira', Deira being an early kingdom roughly corresponding to the East Riding. Bede, who knew Bishop John personally, tells us of his holy life and miracles, and says that when he became too old to continue as bishop, he retired to the monastery, where he died and was buried in the year 721. Almost certainly John's church stood on the site of the Minster; certainly the site of the black marble slab in front of the nave altar was always regarded as his original tomb, and was in the Middle Ages a focus for pilgrims and for miracles of healing. Nothing is known of John's church, although excavations just south of the Minster in 1979–82 located evidence of occupation (possibly monastic) between about 700 and 850.

Nothing very certain is known of the Minster for 300 years after John's death.

Later traditions spoke of a sack by the Vikings, and of the church's refoundation as a college of canons by King Athelstan (924–39). Firmer ground is reached just before the Norman Conquest. Archbishop Aelfric secured John's canonization as St John of Beverley (1037), and he and his successors enlarged and decorated the church: Archbishop Ealdred, who crowned William the Conqueror, built a new presbytery (choir) which may have been modelled on Westminster Abbey, making it the earliest 'Norman' church in northern England. So many pilgrims flocked to John's tomb that a flourishing market town grew up on the north side of the church. By the 12th century the church had the wealth and status that it retained right through to the Reformation: the archbishop of York was lord of the town, but the Minster was controlled by a provost and seven (later eight) canons, who enjoyed great wealth, particularly from a generous royal grant of corn (4 thraves – 316 pounds (143kg) – from every plough in the East Riding). The church's privileges included sanctuary rights for fugitives, not only within the church but throughout the town, and the remains of three sanctuary crosses still stand alongside roads leading into Beverley. The Minster also housed the banner of St John, which was credited with victorious powers in battle from at least 1138 (when it was displayed at a victory over the Scots near Northallerton), and which was frequently borrowed by kings to take on campaign. Edward I did so, for example, on his Scottish campaigns, and made generous gifts to the Minster in return. Later, John's cult received a further boost when Henry V won the battle of Agincourt (1415) on one of his feast days, and made John one of the patron saints of the royal family.

It is likely that the Minster continued to be rebuilt in the new Norman style between the 1060s and 1170s; certainly it retains its Norman font as well as much re-used Norman stone. But in 1188 a fire badly damaged the church, and in about 1213 the central tower collapsed. So, apparently in the 1220s (we have very few firm dates for the Minster), the present church was started at the east end, in the style we now call Early English. Building proceeded rapidly, and all the eastern parts of the Minster – retrochoir, choir, two pairs of transepts, crossing, and the first bay of the nave – were completed by about 1260–70. St John's relics were transferred to a new shrine behind the high altar soon after 1300, and the beautiful reredos (stone screen) was built to carry it. By 1311 work had restarted on the nave, but interestingly the designers chose to adapt the Early English style of the eastern parts rather than to build in the latest Decorated style – and this stroke of genius makes the building a harmonious whole, especially when viewed from inside. The nave took longer to build than the choir, and was completed only in the 1390s. The western towers and north porch were added soon after 1400 in the Perpendicular style; no attempt was made to build a new central tower, presumably because of the spongy ground and the problem of foundations. The medieval church was now complete, except for the additions of the Northumberland Chapel in about 1490, and the choir-stalls in around 1520.

In 1548 the college of canons was suppressed, and most of the church revenues were seized by the government. The chapter house was demolished, and the whole fabric became badly neglected. Fortunately Nicholas Hawksmoor carried out a major restoration between 1717 and 1731, and his collaborator, William Thornton, literally saved the north transept from collapse (see engraving on page 9). Another major restoration was carried out by Sir George Gilbert Scott between 1866 and 1878, and Canon Nolloth (Vicar from 1880–1921) installed many new furnishings including stained-glass windows, the peal of bells, the statues on the West Front, towers and porch, and the wrought-iron railings round the churchyard. Thanks to those

Below right: ①
The Great West Door, with part of the splendidly decorated west front. The carved decoration round the doorway, like that at St Mary Redcliffe, Bristol, may derive from medieval trading links with Spain and Portugal. The statues were added from 1897.

Below (and detail):
The vertical sundials on the south-west tower.

Now or When

restorations the Minster has not only been saved but has been endowed with fine Georgian, Victorian and Edwardian fittings and furnishings to fill the gaps left by destruction and decay. A further restoration and cleaning programme (1975–86) and overhaul of the organ (1994–95) have put the Minster into good repair to continue to serve future generations.

A tour of the Minster, if time and weather allow, should begin outside, starting with the earliest parts at the east end. Walking clockwise, along the south side, is especially rewarding because much of this side is not hemmed in by buildings, and the harmonious blend of styles – Early English eastern arm, Decorated nave and Perpendicular western towers – is seen to best advantage. The effects of medieval

Above:
Doorway to the south façade of the greater transept. The round-headed arch here is, like the rest of this magnificent façade, pure Early English.

subsidence are also clear – the east wall of the south transept is visibly leaning outwards. The earliest stonework is of oolitic limestone from local quarries, but the bulk of the building is of magnesian limestone from the Tadcaster area, and fortunately the Georgian restorers had access to second-hand supplies of the same stone (from St Mary's Abbey, York). However, what is unusual among major churches is that much of the external stone at Beverley is original and not restoration.

The exterior reveals the cathedral scale of the building. It is about 365 feet (111m) long externally, and it has double transepts copied (like much else in the 13th-century parts) from Lincoln. All that is lacking for the complete Gothic scheme is a proper central tower: the present very low one was added by Hawksmoor in 1721 (it was originally crowned by a dome). There are flying buttresses round

Above: ⑤
One of four label-stop carvings apparently depicting illnesses: this one seems to depict stomach-ache.

Left: ⑩
The nave, looking east. It shows to fine effect the elegant Decorated nave harmoniously blending into the Early English chancel.

Below: ⑨
The tread-wheel crane, used to operate a winch let down through the (removable) great boss over the principal crossing.

Above: ⑤
Another Decorated
label-stop – toothache.
(See also pp 14–15.)

Below, right: ⑪
A contemporary
engraving showing the
shoring of the north
front of the great
transept by Thornton of
York. A column within
leans to this day.

the whole building except the north transept, and these were necessary to carry the thrust of the stone vaults down to the ground. The details of doors, windows, buttresses, parapets, gables and turrets are worth studying, including the rose windows of the main transepts, and the worn sculptures on the parapets of the nave aisles. Three medieval statues survive on the exterior: St John and King Athelstan on either side of the great east window, and a man in armour, said to represent Henry Percy, first Earl of Northumberland, just above Queen Victoria on the north-west tower. Remains of the demolished church of St Martin, once a separate parish church, can be seen between the two sundials at the south-west corner of the church. Finally, the west front with its twin towers is superb – in the view of Alec Clifton-Taylor it surpasses all English cathedral west fronts as an architectural composition. The north tower houses a peal of 10 bells, cast by Taylors of Loughborough in 1901; in the south tower are 'Great John' (another Taylor bell of 1901) and two medieval bells, 'Peter' (currently used as the prayer bell) and 'Brithunus'.

It should be realized that the medieval Minster was surrounded by other buildings forming a close – the chapter house, dormitory, refectory, canons' houses, and so on – but none of them survive any longer except, perhaps, embedded in some of the older houses in St John Street. Hall Garth, the open field south of the nave, is the site of the palace which was used by the medieval archbishops of York when they stayed in Beverley.

The usual entrance is through the two-storeyed Highgate porch, added in the early 15th century to make an imposing entrance from the town. Once inside, the most rewarding procedure is to leave the splendid nave until later, and to proceed at once to the earlier, eastern parts. Notice as you go the lofty proportions, which seem even higher than they are because the main roof vault of the eastern parts is 100 feet (30m) high, and the chancel and main transepts only 27 feet (8m) wide. Such proportions make it look more French than most great English churches, and 'although direct French influences are unlikely, Beverley comes nearer than any other example of the Early English style to the . . . beauty of Soissons or Amiens' (Christopher Wilson, *The Gothic Cathedral*).

We start in the retrochoir behind the high altar, where the present building was begun. Like all the eastern parts, it is in the Early English style, characterized by pointed arches, lancet windows, 'stiff-leaf' foliage capitals, and many columns of dark, polished Purbeck marble from Dorset. The 14th-century reredos has beautiful patterned carving and figure sculpture, including musicians. In good light, or with a torch, you can find medieval and Tudor graffiti, including ships, on the flat face inside the arches, probably

dating from the time when the retrochoir was used as a grammar school. The great east window, inserted shortly after 1416, now includes most of the medieval stained glass which survived the Reformation. The lower part includes 21 small scenes of 13th-century date, depicting episodes from the lives of St Martin, St Nicholas, and possibly St Leonard. Other glass, including the large figures in the lower half, is 14th-century, while the upper half of the window retains much of the original glass of c.1416–20. The retrochoir also houses some fine monuments of the 17th to 19th centuries, mostly of members of the local families of Warton and Pennyman. That of Sir Michael Warton (who died in 1725), signed by the great sculptor Scheemakers, is especially fine, though it is placed in uncompromising fashion just where an eastern altar would originally have stood, perhaps out of respect for his major part in funding the Minster's restoration.

The retrochoir was designed to fit into a processional route which ran right round the interior (see the Visitors' Guide on the inside front cover). However, St Katherine's Chapel to the south is now reserved for private prayer, and the south choir aisle has been blocked off for the organ; so we proceed west via the north choir aisle, glancing first at the Northumberland Chapel (number 21 on the plan), added to house the tomb of Henry Percy, 4th Earl of Northumberland, who was murdered by rebels in 1489. The Percys were the dominant local aristocrats in the 14th and 15th centuries, living nearby at Leconfield, and a little further west (number 15 on the plan) stands another Percy tomb. There is no effigy, and it is not even certain which Percy lady it commemorates. Lady Eleanor, who died in 1328, is the most likely candidate, though if so the tomb must have been completed later, since the heraldry demands a date after 1339. However, what is important is that

we have here the finest British tomb of its time, finer even than anything to be found in Westminster Abbey; and, astonishingly, its lovely carvings of Christ and supporting angels were not destroyed at the Reformation (see pages 14 and 15). Its decoration is easier to appreciate than to describe in words, but notice the three-dimensional effect of the 'nodding' arches.

The Percy Tomb is best viewed from the south side, so we step through some lovely 18th-century wrought-iron gates and turn left into the choir. Once inside, the Early English architecture is seen in all its glory, with its three storeys (arcades, triforium, clerestory) crowned by a stone vault. The 13th-century designers must have enjoyed playing with patterns and shapes: observe, for example, how the blank arcading in the triforium is doubled to create a 'syncopated' rhythm, and how the four great piers of the east crossing overhang at the top. Above this east crossing, but visible only from the roof, are traces of what may have been an abandoned attempt to build an eastern tower. The reredos behind the high altar is much altered from this side – it was

Above: ⑳
The choir looking east, showing the *trompe l'oeil* effect of the Georgian flooring. Beyond is the Perpendicular (*c.*1417) Great East Window.

Left: ⑳
One of Beverley Minster's 68 misericords.

Facing page: ⑩
James Elwell of Beverley made this sumptuous pulpitum to the design of Sir George Gilbert Scott. The parapet niches hold statues of Athelstan, St Nicholas, St Mary, St John the Evangelist, St Martin and St John of Beverley.

largely renewed in 1826, and covered with statues and mosaics in 1897 – but between the reredos and the Percy Tomb stands the oldest surviving object in the Minster, the so-called 'frith stool'. It is traditionally linked to the Minster's right of sanctuary (frithu is the Anglo-Saxon word for 'peace'), but may have been originally a bishop's or abbot's throne. Altogether the choir is full of good furnishings, including 14th-century wooden sedilia (the seats to the south of the altar), 18th-century marble flooring with a *trompe l'oeil* (deceives the eye) pattern (see above), and Victorian ceiling paintings by Scott in the style of the 13th-century. The sedilia cleverly echo the nodding arches of the Percy Tomb opposite, and may well have been designed by the same hand. Best of all are the choir-stalls, constructed in about 1520. The oak canopies, with their tiny vaults, have been much restored,

The North Choir Aisle

and some of the heads and figures on canopies and bench-ends are Georgian or Victorian; but the medieval bench-ends include a fine elephant and castle (for Queen Catherine of Aragon?) on the south side. Underneath the seats are 68 misericords (carved scenes on tip-up seats), more than in any English cathedral. Unfortunately, the seats are now fragile and permission is needed to view them, but they are notable for their portrayal of very realistic farmyard scenes. The choir is terminated to the west by the organ and organ screen, but these will be better viewed from the nave.

First, however, it is worthwhile returning to the Percy Tomb to continue west along the north choir aisle; the best feature here is the double staircase which once led to the doors of the demolished chapter house. Opposite the staircase are modern notice boards listing the provosts, vicars and organists of the Minster; one famous name included, though he never lived in Beverley, is Thomas Becket, provost *c*.1153–62 (the dates given are not quite accurate), who later became the archbishop of Canterbury, saint and martyr. Then we proceed through a stone doorway into the north transept. Both transepts are spacious, each with two aisles, and their architecture is beautifully restrained Early English – 'the Beverley system in its greatest purity' in the judgement of Sir Nikolaus Pevsner. The north transept was on the point of collapse when Thornton pushed the north wall back into place with a giant wooden frame; even today the north-east pillar visibly leans out of true. The finest monument in the north transept is the priest's tomb (number 12 on the plan), almost certainly that of Provost Nicholas de Huggate who died in 1338. His effigy is beautifully carved with mass vestments decorated with heraldic shields, which helped to identify him; the tomb-chest may well be from another monument,

probably the tomb canopy in the nave.

Before turning to the nave, it is best to complete the 13th-century parts by proceeding via the main crossing (number 9 on the plan) into the south transept. The crossing space is usually occupied by the circular movable altar (1970), and this

Left: ⑮
This detail on the Percy Tomb shows Christ enthroned receiving the soul of the departed (Lady Eleanor Percy?).

Below and below, ⑤ right:
Two more of the Decorated label-stops (see also pp 8–9). These are said to represent lumbago and sciatica.

Above: ⑮
Percy Tomb detail, showing angels bearing a crown (on the soffit of the canopy to the east).

Right: ⑮
The Percy Tomb is traditionally attributed to Lady Eleanor Fitz Alan, wife of Henry de Percy, the first Lord Percy of Alnwick. The ornate freestone canopy in the Decorated style is unsurpassed in quality, a crowning achievement of medieval European art.

Left: ⑯
An intricately carved boss in the Decorated style on the underside of the reredos vaulting of a Green Man, a symbol of fertility.

The Nave

Left: (17)
The so-called Frith Stool or chair of peace. It is probably an Anglo-Saxon bishop's or abbot's throne, possibly even connected with St John himself. Later, it may have been used by the official investigating fugitives' pleas for sanctuary.

partly covers another fine 18th-century pavement. If we stand west of the altar rail, we have a good view of the intricate wooden choir-screen of 1878–80, designed by Scott to match the choir-stalls, and carved by James Elwell of Beverley. It is surmounted by Johann Snetzler's superb organ of 1769, housed in a case of 1916 designed by Arthur Hill. Such a vintage instrument has had to be repaired and partly reconstructed more than once (notably by Thomas Hill in 1885, and by Wood of Huddersfield in 1994–95), but thanks to sympathetic restoration it retains more Snetzler pipe-work than any other organ. Looking up to the ceiling of the central tower, we see a circular boss in richly painted wood, directly above the nave altar; this is removable, to allow for the use of a hoist in the tower for raising building materials. Those joining a guided tour of the roofs can see the massive tread-wheel which used to operate the hoist, of medieval origin though largely reconstructed. The south transept, though architecturally fine, has few outstanding furnishings except for the military memorials in the eastern chapels. The central chapel has a cenotaph (designed by F. L. Pearson in 1921) commemorating the men of the East Yorkshire Regiment who died in the First World War, and modelled on the tomb of King Edward the Confessor in Westminster Abbey, while in the other chapels hang old Colours of the regiment. On the south wall is a 17th-century painting in primitive style, depicting King Athelstan handing St John a charter of privileges – a charming yet historically impossible scene; and on one pillar is a carved bracket which may have held St John's banner.

Finally, we move into the nave, where a good starting point is the modern floor-slab marking the tomb of St John (see number 8 on the plan); here is the very origin of Minster and town. The tomb is decorated annually with primroses brought by the children from nearby Harpham, traditionally regarded as John's birthplace. It is a good spot from which to study the transition from the first bay of the nave to the later work further west; the general style and proportions remained unchanged, though the nave windows are in the new Decorated style (and Perpendicular further west), and in the north aisle the wall arcading is in full 14th-century style. Nevertheless, such respect for a style of the past is rare among the greater English medieval churches. The most exquisite features of the nave are perhaps the carvings of men, women and angels playing musical instruments, masking the junctions just above the nave pillars, and – at a more easily visible level – the figures at the junctions of the arcades in the north aisle. Some are comical or grotesque, but the most unusual are a great array of musicians. Altogether there are over 70 medieval carved figures in the Minster playing musical instruments – there are said to be more in Beverley Minster than in any other European church – but no-one knows why. One other feature of the nave which is not visible except, again, by a visit to the roof – the vault is no longer of stone but of brick, a remarkably early use of such a material in England, and a century earlier than Beverley's North Bar of 1409.

Above:
An early 19th-century drawing of a sanctuary cross.

Right: (14)
In the foreground are the 18th-century gates formerly at the entrance to the choir. The fine Early English double stair on the right originally gave access via a double door to a raised 13th-century octagonal Chapter House (demolished 1550). The door under the landing led to the sacristy.

The nave and nave aisles have their fair share of interesting features. The earliest are the Norman font, a huge piece of Frosterley marble from County Durham, and, a little further east, a 14th-century tomb canopy traditionally called the 'two sisters' tomb', though it is not known who was buried there. However, the best furnishings are Georgian and Victorian, an especially interesting combination because, while many medieval churches were first Georgianised and later on Victorianised, the Victorians normally obliterated the Georgian fittings. To some extent this happened at Beverley too – the Georgian pews, galleries and choir screen were all removed by the Victorians,

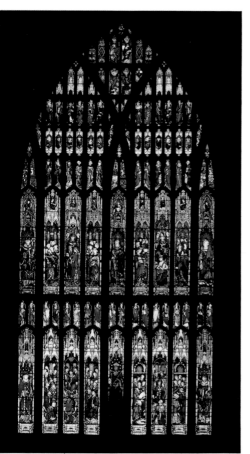

though the two splendid painted lead figures of John and Athelstan from the choir screen were spared, and now stand on either side of the nave south doors. Much Georgian woodwork was also spared – the south doors are Georgian, as are the splendid great west doors, with their effigies of the Four Evangelists and their symbols: from left to right, the eagle (St John), ox (St Luke), lion (St Mark) and angel (St Matthew). Even finer is the font cover of 1726, with cherubs' heads, scrolls, and a dove, and topped by rich ironwork of 1762 – a piece as good as anything in Wren's London churches. Notice also, behind the font and in the next bay east, the aisle windows: they look identical to the windows further east, but they are in fact Georgian insertions where originally the church of St Martin joined on to the Minster. They remind us how the Georgian restorers worked in sympathy with the style of the building. The Victorian and Edwardian restorers contributed to the nave the brass lectern, the stone statues at the west end, and a fine set of stained-glass windows, most of

Above: ①
The carved oak figures on the Great West Door represent the four evangelists Matthew, Mark, Luke and John (from right to left) with their symbols beneath. The doors were designed by William Thornton of York, and possibly carved by his assistants.

Left: ①
The Great West Window is Perpendicular in style, like the Great East Window. The Victorian stained glass portraying scenes of the early history of Christianity in Northumbria was designed by Hardman and installed by public subscription (1859–61).

Above: ②
The Norman font of
Frosterley marble, with
its splendid 18th-century
wooden cover carved by
the Thorntons. The cast-
lead figures of St John
of Beverley and King
Athelstan can be seen
on the right.

them by the firms of Hardman & Co., and
Clayton and Bell. Despite the effect of the
stained glass, the nave remains an airy
and well-lit space in which to end a visit.
It is also a good place to sit and reflect on
the beauty and proportions of the whole
building, and to appreciate that this
beauty depends on careful design and not
accident: a recent study of the Minster

has found that the medieval designers
employed a very coherent system of mea-
surements and proportions. The techni-
calities need not be grasped to appreciate
the results. The visitor may well feel that,
in the words of J. E. Morris, the writer of
several guidebooks to Yorkshire at the
beginning of this century, the Minster is
'the most beautiful building in Yorkshire'.